979.4   Grabowski, John F
Gra   The Pacific

50581

DATE DUE   PERMA-BOUND

D0786529

STATE REPORTS

The Pacific

CALIFORNIA ★ HAWAII

By
John F. Grabowski
Patricia A. Grabowski

CHELSEA HOUSE PUBLISHERS

New York   Philadelphia

Produced by James Charlton Associates
New York, New York.

First Printing

1   3   5   7   9   8   6   4   2

Library of Congress Cataloging-in-Publication Data

Grabowski, John F.
    The Pacific: California, Hawaii / by John Grabowski,
Patricia Grabowski.
    p. cm. — (State reports)
    Summary: Discusses the geographical, historical, and cultural aspects of
California and Hawaii. Includes bibliographical references and index.
    ISBN 0-7910-1050-3
        0-7910-1397-9 (pbk.)
    1. Pacific States—Juvenile literature. 2. California—Juvenile literature.
3. Hawaii—Juvenile literature. [1. Pacific States. 2. California. 3. Hawaii.]
I. Grabowski, Patricia. II. Title. III. Series: Aylesworth, Thomas G. State reports.

F851.G75 1992   91-18941
979.4—dc20   CIP
                                          AC

Contents

California

Hawaii

California

The state seal of California was first adopted in 1849. Since then it has been redesigned, with the present seal adopted in 1937. Minerva, the Roman goddess of wisdom, war, arts, and handicrafts, is seated. The bear in front of Minerva's shield is a symbol of the early American settlers' struggle for independence and, as such, is a reminder of the bear flag revolt of 1846. Ships in the background represent commerce; a sheaf of wheat and clusters of grapes stand for agriculture. The Sierra Nevada mountains are pictured in the distance and a miner at work can be seen on the shore. The state motto appears beneath a semi-circle of 31 stars, representing the number of states in the Union after the admission of California. Printed around the outer circle are the words The Great Seal of the State of California.

State Flag

The state flag of California was adopted in 1911. In the center of a white field is a brown grizzly bear on a patch of green grass. A horizontal red stripe runs along the bottom of the flag, with "California Republic" printed above it. A five-pointed star, representing sovereignty, appears in the upper left corner. The colors of the flag are symbolic; white standing for purity and red for courage.

State Motto

Eureka

The Greek motto, meaning "I have found it," refers to the state's admission to the Union and to the discovery of gold.

A view of the Santa Monica Beach in Southern California.

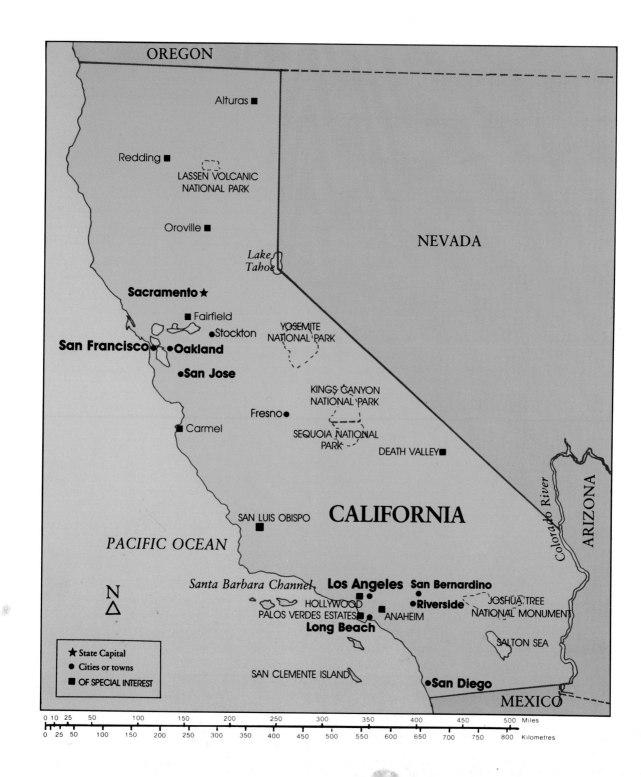

OREGON

Alturas ■

Redding ■

LASSEN VOLCANIC
NATIONAL PARK

NEVADA

Oroville ■

*Lake
Tahoe*

Sacramento ★

■ Fairfield

YOSEMITE
NATIONAL PARK

●Stockton

San Francisco● ●**Oakland**

●**San Jose**

KINGS CANYON
NATIONAL PARK

Fresno●

● Carmel

SEQUOIA NATIONAL
PARK

DEATH VALLEY■

CALIFORNIA

ARIZONA

Colorado River

SAN LUIS OBISPO
■

PACIFIC OCEAN

Santa Barbara Channel **Los Angeles** **San Bernardino**

N
△

HOLLYWOOD
PALOS VERDES ESTATES■
●**Riverside**

JOSHUA TREE
NATIONAL MONUMENT

■ANAHEIM

Long Beach

SALTON SEA

★ State Capital
● Cities or towns
■ OF SPECIAL INTEREST

SAN CLEMENTE ISLAND

●**San Diego**

MEXICO

| 0 10 25 | 50 | 100 | 150 | 200 | 250 | 300 | 350 | 400 | 450 | 500 | Miles |

| 0 25 50 | 100 | 150 | 200 | 250 | 300 | 350 | 400 | 450 | 500 | 550 | 600 | 650 | 700 | 750 | 800 | Kilometres |

The California State Capitol was built from 1860-1874, in the Classic Revival style. It underwent extensive renovations in 1976.

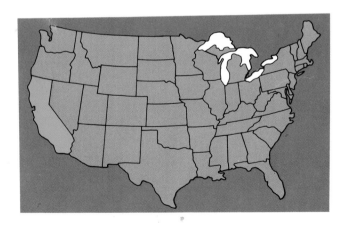

State Capital

Sacramento has been the state capital since 1854. Prior to that, Monterey, San Jose, Vallejo, Benecia, and San Francisco were used briefly as capitals. Construction of a permanent capitol building began in 1860. It was completed in 1874, and subsequently remodeled in 1906-08 and 1928. Between 1976 and 1981, the building was completely restored at a cost of $68 million. The four-story structure, built of granite and stuccoed brick, is Roman Corinthian in design. The copper-clad dome reaches a height of almost 220 feet. Rising from the dome is a gold-plated cupola supporting a 30-inch copper ball, which has been plated with gold coins. Between 1949 and 1952, a six-story annex was added to the building at a cost of $7.6 million.

State Name and Nickname

Spanish explorers named California after an imaginary island in a 16th-century novel, *The Deeds of Esplandián,* by Garci Ordoñez de Montalvo.

The official nickname of California, *The Golden State,* was chosen in 1968. It refers to the discovery of gold at Sutter's mill in 1848, to the fields of yellow poppies that bloom in the spring, and to California's brilliant sunshine.

State Fish

In 1947, the California golden trout, *Salmo aquabonita,* was named state fish.

State Tree

California redwood, *Sequoia sempervirens* and *Sequoia gigantea,* were designated state trees in 1937.

State Bird

The California valley quail, *Lophortyx californica,* was selected state bird by popular vote in 1931.

State Animal

The California grizzly bear, *Ursus californicus,* was chosen state animal in 1953.

State Flower

The state legislature designated the golden poppy, *Eschscholtzia californica,* state flower in 1903.

State Fossil

The California saber-toothed cat, *Smilodon californicus,* was named state fossil in 1973.

State Insect

In 1972, the California dogface butterfly, *Zerene eurydice,* was chosen state insect.

State Marine Mammal

The California gray whale, *Eschrichtius robustus,* was designated state marine mammal in 1975.

State Mineral

Gold was selected state mineral in 1965.

State Reptile

In 1972, the California desert tortoise, *Gopherus agassizi,* was chosen state reptile.

State Rock

Serpentine was named state rock in 1965.

State Song

"I Love You, California," with words by F. B. Silverwood and music by A. F. Frankenstein, is the state song of California. Although it was first introduced in 1913, it was not officially adopted by the state legislature until 1951.

The brightly colored golden poppy is the state flower.

Population

The population of California in 1990 was 29,839,250, making it the most populous state in the nation. There are 188.0 people per square mile—91.3 percent of the population live in towns and cities. About 85 percent of the residents of California were born in the United States.

Geography and Climate

Bounded on the north by Oregon, on the east by Nevada and Arizona, on the south by Mexico, and on the west by the Pacific Ocean, California has an area of 158,706 square miles, making it the third largest state. The climate is variable, with moderate temperatures and rainfall along the coast, and extremes in the interior. California has a long, mountainous coastline, a central valley, the Sierra Nevada mountains in the east, desert basins in the southern interior, and rugged mountains in the north. The highest point, at 14,494 feet, is Mount Whitney in the Sierra Nevada, while the lowest point, at 282 feet below sea level, is only 80 miles away at Badwater in Death Valley. These are also the highest and lowest points in the entire United States outside of Alaska. The major waterways in California are the American, Colorado, Eel, Feather, Kern, Klamath, Mad, Merced, Mokelumne, Russian, Sacramento, Salinas, Salmon, San Joaquin, Trinity, and Tuolumne rivers. Lake Tahoe is the deepest lake in the state, while the largest natural lake within California is Clear Lake.

Industries

The principal industries of the state are agriculture, services, manufacturing, and trade. The chief manufactured products are foods, primary and fabricated metals, machinery, electric and electronic equipment, and transportation equipment.

Agriculture

The chief crops of the state are grapes, cotton, oranges,

An elaborate sand castle dominates the landscape at this San Diego beach.

hay, tomatoes, lettuce, strawberries, almonds, broccoli, walnuts, sugar beets, peaches, and potatoes. California is also a livestock state, and there are estimated to be 4.9 million cattle and calves, 140,000 hogs and pigs, 955,000 sheep, and 281.5 million chickens and turkeys on its farms. Fir, pine, redwood, and oak are harvested for timber. Asbestos, boron minerals, cement, diatomite, calcined, gypsum, construction sand and gravel are important mineral products. Commercial fishing brings in $123.3 million per year.

Government

The governor of California is elected to a four-year term, as are the lieutenant governor, secretary of state, attorney general, treasurer, controller, and superintendent of public instruction. The voters also elect a five-member State Board of Equalization. The state legislature, whose sessions begin in even-numbered years and last for two years, consists of a 40-member senate and an 80-member assembly. Senators serve four-year terms and are elected from senatorial districts; assembly members serve two-year terms and are elected from assembly districts. The most recent state constitution was adopted in 1879. In addition to its two U.S. senators, California has 52 representatives in the U.S. House of Representatives.

The state has 54 votes in the electoral college.

History

As many as 300,000 Indians lived in California before the arrival of the Europeans. The Hupa inhabited the northwestern part of the state, the Maidu the central section, and the Yuma the south. Lake, Mendocino, and Sonoma counties were occupied by the Pomo Indians. Other groups in the area were the Míwok, Modoc, and Mojave tribes.

The first European to see the Pacific coast was Juan Rodríguez Cabrillo, a Portuguese navigator sailing for Spain. He explored San Diego Bay in 1542. In 1579, Sir Francis Drake, an English sea captain, sailed along the coast and claimed the land for England, naming it New Albion. After discovering the

The Hupa Indians lived on the Pacific coast for many centuries before being pushed out by the expansion of the United States.

bay of Monterey during his voyage of 1602, Sebastián Vizcaíno strongly urged Spain to colonize California. Although the Spaniards established missions and settlements in Baja California—now a part of Mexico—in 1697, it was not until 1769 that Gaspar de Portolá, the governor of Baja California, led a land expedition up the California coast and founded the first presidio, or military fort, at San Diego. During this expedition Father Junípero Serra established San Diego de Alcalá, the first California mission. By 1823, twenty-one missions had been built northward by the Franciscans, each one about a day's walk from the next.

For a short time the Russians, who had fur trading settlements in Alaska, moved south into California. Fort Ross was built in 1812 about 60 miles north of San Francisco, but was abandoned in 1841.

California became part of

Father Junípero Serra helped found nine Franciscan missions in California between 1769-1782.

Mexico in 1821 when Mexico gained its independence from Spain. By 1831, the governor was forced to return to Mexico City, thus weakening Mexican control over the region. When American settlers arrived in California during the 1840s, the United States offered to buy the land, but Mexico refused. In 1845, Captain John C. Frémont, a United States Army officer and explorer, incurred the distrust of the Mexicans when he led two surveying parties into California. He broke the peace and, in 1846, encouraged a group of American settlers to take over Mexico's headquarters in Sonoma. This incident became known as the Bear Flag Revolt after the settlers raised a flag bearing a single star, a grizzly bear, and the words "California Republic" over the fort. The Mexican War ended in 1848 with the signing of the Treaty of Guadalupe Hidalgo, by which Mexico ceded California to the United

John Augustus Sutter owned the famous Sutter's Mill that created the gold rush of the late 1840s. Bankrupted by goldseekers, Sutter moved to Pennsylvania in 1873.

States. California was admitted to the Union as the 31st state on September 9, 1850.

In 1848, shortly before the peace treaty was signed, gold was found at a sawmill owned by John A. Sutter. News of this discovery spread quickly, and thousands of people rushed to California to establish their claims. These "forty-niners," as they were called, greatly increased the population of the region.

By 1870, there were about 560,000 people living in the state. Agriculture and industry increased in importance, and the population continued its steady growth into the early 1900s.

The completion of the Panama Canal in 1914 added to California's development, since it shortened the sea route between California and the eastern states.

World War I brought the construction of shipyards, rubber plants, and other factories to assist the war effort. The Great Depression of the 1930s saw California suffer economically, though not as severely as most other states. With the onset of World War II, the state became the nation's aircraft center, producing airplanes, ships, and weapons. This marked the beginning of a period of remarkable economic prosperity, which has continued to the present day.

Sports

California is a hotbed of sports activity. On the collegiate level, the NCAA baseball championship has been won by the University of California (1947, 1957), USC (1948, 1958, 1961, 1963, 1968, 1970-74, 1978), Cal State Fullerton (1979, 1984), and Stanford University (1987-88). In basketball, Stanford (1942), University of San Francisco (1955-56), California (1959), and UCLA (1964-65, 1967-73, 1975) have won the NCAA tournament, while San Francisco (1949), Fresno State University (1983), and UCLA (1985) have won the National Invitation Tournament. Football's Rose Bowl game is held in Pasadena every year. California, USC, Stanford, and UCLA have each won several times over the years. Santa Clara University has triumphed in the Orange Bowl (1950) and the Sugar Bowl (1937-38), while St.

Mary's was victorious in the Cotton Bowl in 1939.

On the professional level, California is represented by numerous teams in the four major sports. In baseball, the Los Angeles Dodgers play their home games in Dodger Stadium, the San Diego Padres in San Diego/Jack Murphy Stadium, the San Francisco Giants in Candlestick Park, the Oakland Athletics in the Oakland Coliseum, and the California Angels in Anaheim Stadium, which they share with the Los Angeles Rams of the National Football League. The NFL's Los Angeles Raiders play in the Memorial Coliseum, while the San Francisco 49ers play in Candlestick Park and the San Diego Chargers in San Diego/Jack Murphy Stadium. National Basketball Association teams based in California include the Los Angeles Lakers, who play in the Great Western Forum, the Los Angeles Clippers (Memorial Sports Arena), the Golden State Warriors (Oakland Coliseum Arena), and the Sacramento Kings (ARCO Arena). The Los Angeles Kings of the National Hockey League also perform in the Great Western Forum, while the San Jose Sharks will play in the Cow Palace when they enter the league for the 1991-92 season.

Major Cities

Los Angeles (population 2,966,850). In 1781, Don Felipe de Neve, Governor of California, founded El Pueblo de Nuestra Señora La Reina de Los Angeles de Porciuncula—"The Town of Our Lady the Queen of the Angels of Porciuncula." With the seizure of California by the United States in 1846, the town was transformed into a thriving frontier community. Its growth received a tremendous boost from the gold rush of 1849. The population doubled

The Rose Bowl, one of the most important games in college football, is held annually at Pasadena, California.

Hollywood's Sunset Strip is one of the most famous streets in the country.

in the 1920s, setting the stage for even greater growth in the years to come, and by 1940 it had surpassed the 1.5 million mark. This expansion continues to the present day, as the sprawling metropolis has become a major scientific, artistic, and cultural community.

Places to visit in Los Angeles: City Hall, Music Center of Los Angeles County, Los Angeles Children's Museum, Museum of Contemporary Art, Wells Fargo History Museum, Little Tokyo, Chinatown, Los Angeles Temple Visitors Center, El Pueblo de Los Angeles Historic Park, Avila Adobe, Old Plaza Firehouse, Olvera Street, Sepulveda House (1887), Griffith Park, Los Angeles Zoo, UCLA Botanical Garden, Elysian Park, Descanso Gardens, Los Angeles State and County Arboretum, Exposition Park, Los Angeles Memorial Coliseum, Natural History Museum of Los Angeles County, California Museum of Science and Industry, Lummis Home and Garden State Historical Monument, Southwest Museum, South Coast Botanic Garden, Farmers Market, Will Rogers State Historic Park, Los Angeles County Museum of Art, George C. Page La Brea Discoveries Museum, Rancho La Brea Tar Pits, CBS Television City, Paramount Film and Television Studios, Simon Rodia Towers, Wight Art Gallery, and the Junior Arts Center.

Sacramento (population 338,220). Sacramento was settled in 1839 by Captain John Sutter on a 50,000-acre land grant from the Mexican government. The present-day city was laid out on Sutter's property in 1848. When gold was found on the land that same year, the city rapidly grew into a major supply center. It was chosen state capital in 1854.

Places to visit in Sacramento: State Capitol, California Vietnam Veterans Memorial, Crocker Art Museum, Old Governor's Mansion, Old Sacramento Historic District, B. F. Hastings Museum,

California State Railroad Museum, Central Pacific Railroad Station Museum, Old Eagle Theatre, Sacramento History Center, Sacramento Science Center, State Archives, State Library, Sutter's Fort State Historic Park, State Indian Museum, Towe Ford Museum, Waterworld USA, Fairytale Town, and the Sacramento Zoo.

San Diego (population 875,538). Founded in 1769 by Gaspar de Portolá, California's southernmost city is just across the border from Mexico. Growth in the area was slow until after California achieved statehood in 1850. In recent years, San Diego has become a major metropolitan center, as well as a popular year-round resort city. It is the home of the 11th Naval District, and a center for electronics, manufacturing, education, health and biomedical research, and ship, aircraft, and missile building.

Places to visit in San Diego: Mission Basilica San Diego de Alcalá, Presidio Park, Junípero Serra Museum, Whaley House (1856), Old Town San Diego State Historic Park, Gaslamp Quarter, Balboa Park, San Diego Zoo, Natural History Museum, Reuben H. Fleet Space Theater and Science Center, San Diego Aerospace Museum, International Aerospace Hall of Fame, San Diego Museum of Art, Timken Art Gallery, Museum of Photographic Arts, San Diego Hall of Champions, Museum of Man, Old Globe Theatre, Spanish Village Arts and Crafts Center, Seaport Village, Villa Montezuma/ Jesse Shepard House (1887), Sea World, Embarcadero, Mission Bay Park, and San Diego Wild Animal Park.

San Francisco (population 678,974). Founded in 1776 by the Spanish, San Francisco is an "air-conditioned city," with warm winters and cool summers. The discovery of gold at Sutter's mill in 1848 had a tremendous impact on the growth of the city. It became an important port and supply depot for miners in their search for gold, with its population blossoming from 800 in 1848 to 25,000 the following year. Despite suffering millions of dollars in damage caused by a devastating earthquake in 1906, the city has continued to prosper. Today, San Francisco is an important financial center and a melting pot of cultures from around the world.

Balboa Park in San Diego encompasses 1,400 acres and is the location for many of the city's museums, as well as the San Diego Zoo.

Places to visit in San Francisco:
Twin Peaks, Mission Dolores (1776), City Hall, Performing Arts Center, War Memorial/ Opera House, Cow Palace, Haas-Lilienthal House (1886), Japan Center, Golden Gate Bridge, Palace of Fine Arts, Acres of Orchids, Cable Car Museum, Society of California Pioneers Museum and Library, San Francisco Museum of Modern Art, Wells Fargo Bank History Museum, Treasure Island Museum, Randall Museum, National Maritime Museum, Exploratorium, California Palace of Legion of Honor, M. H. de Young Memorial Museum, Asian Art Museum, California Academy of Sciences, Natural History Museum and Aquarium, Mexican Museum, Old Mint, Alcatraz Island, Embarcadero, Chinatown, Telegraph Hill, Fisherman's Wharf, Presidio, Ghiradelli Square, Pier 39, and San Francisco Zoo.

Home to about thirty fishing vessels, Fisherman's Wharf in San Francisco is a popular visiting spot for seafood-loving tourists.

Places To Visit

The National Park Service maintains 18 areas in the state of California: Cabrillo National Monument, Death Valley National Monument, Devils Postpile National Monument, Joshua Tree National Monument, Lava Beds National Monument, Muir Woods National Monument, Pinnacles National Monument, Channel Islands National Park, Lassen Volcanic National Park, Sequoia and Kings Canyon National Parks, Yosemite National Park, Redwood National Park, Point Reyes National Seashore, Whiskeytown-Shasta-Trinity National Recreation Area, Golden Gate National Recreation Area, John Muir National Historical Site, and Fort Point National Historic Site. In addition, there are 86 state recreation areas.

Alturas: Modoc County Historical Museum. Exhibits include Indian artifacts and an extensive firearms collection.

Anaheim: Disneyland. This 80-acre park is divided into seven main sections: Main Street, USA; Fantasyland; Tomorrowland; Adventureland; Frontierland; New Orleans Square; and, Critter Country.

Arcadia: Los Angeles State and County Arboretum. This horticultural research center contains 127 acres of plants from around the world, as well as several historic buildings.

Auburn: Placer County Museum. Old mining equipment, weapons, and old photographs depict the early days of Placer County.

Bakersfield: Kern County Museum. Visitors may tour this 15-acre village containing many restored buildings, including a Queen Anne mansion, wooden jail, hotel, and saloon.

Barstow: Calico Ghost Town Regional Park. This restored 1880s mining town includes a general store, a schoolhouse, and the Maggie Mine.

Berkeley: Judah L. Magnes Museum. This museum houses artistic, historical, and literary materials tracing Jewish life throughout the world.

Bishop: Laws Railroad Museum and Historical Site.

The sheer face of Half-Dome Mountain in Yosemite National Park (established in 1890) attracts many mountain climbers.

Disneyland is a favorite vacation spot for people of all ages.

Visitors may tour a post office containing vintage equipment and a restored station-agent's house.

Bridgeport: Bodie State Historic Park. Fires in 1892 and 1932 destroyed all but a few buildings in this unrestored, late-1800s ghost town.

Buena Park: Knott's Berry Farm. An Old West Ghost Town, Fiesta Village, Wild Water Wilderness, and Camp Snoopy are featured in California's oldest amusement park.

Calistoga: Old Faithful Geyser of California. This geyser, fed by an underground river, erupts every 40 minutes, sending thousands of gallons of water 60 feet in the air.

Carmel: Mission San Carlos Borromeo del Río Carmelo. Founded in 1770 by Father Junípero Serra, this mission was the priest's home until his death in 1784.

Desert Hot Springs: Cabot's Old Indian Pueblo and Museum. This four-story Hopi Indian-style mansion features Indian and Eskimo artifacts.

Escondido: Lawrence Welk Theatre-Museum. This museum contains mementos from the career of the well-known bandleader.

Fairfield: Western Railway Museum. Visitors may take a two-mile ride on a streetcar, and tour a museum containing 100 antique trains and railroad cars.

Fort Bragg: California Western Railroad. A 40-mile round trip on a train affectionately known as the "Skunk" takes passengers through groves of redwood trees along the Noyo River.

Fremont: Mission San José. This adobe church, reconstructed after the original was destroyed by an earthquake, contains the original baptismal font, statues, and historic vestments.

Fresno: The Discovery Center. This family-oriented museum features hands-on science exhibits and American Indian artifacts.

Garden Grove: Crystal Cathedral. This church, designed by Philip Johnson, resembles a four-pointed crystal star.

Hollywood: Mann's Chinese Theatre. The handprints and footprints of many movie stars can be seen in the cement at the entrance to this theater.

La Jolla: Scripps Aquarium-Museum. This aquarium-museum features a marine life exhibit and an onshore tidepool.

Lompoc: Mission La Purísima Concepción State Historic Park. Indian artifacts and mission relics are displayed in this restored mission, originally founded in 1787.

Long Beach: *Queen Mary.* Visitors may tour the wheelhouse, officer's quarters, salons, and engine room of this historic ship.

Malibu: J. Paul Getty Museum. This recreation of an ancient Roman villa contains Greek and Roman antiquities, and pre-20th-century paintings, drawings, and sculptures.

Marina Del Rey: Fisherman's Village. This is a model of a turn-of-the-century New England fishing village.

Modesto: McHenry Museum. Historical exhibits are displayed in period rooms, including a schoolroom, blacksmith shop, and doctor's office.

Monterey: Monterey State Historic Park. The buildings in this park include the

Many Hollywood actors and actresses hope to have their handprints, footprints, and signatures displayed at the forecourt of Mann's Chinese Theatre, as a symbol of their stardom status.

Robert Louis Stevenson House and California's First Theater.

Morgan Hill: Wagons to Wings Museum. This museum houses wagons, coaches, and planes of various types,

including many one-of-a-kind vehicles.

Oakland: Oakland Museum. This complex of galleries and gardens features exhibits on the natural science, history, and art of California.

Oceanside: Camp Pendleton. This 125,000-acre Marine Corps base serves as an ecological preserve, in addition to being one of the world's leading amphibious training camps.

The Queen Mary, *at one time one of the world's greatest transatlantic cruise ships, is now permanently docked in Long Beach.*

Miniature horses were first introduced in the 16th century, as pets for the royal courts in Europe. The Winners' Circle Ranch is the largest miniature horse ranch in the western U.S.; they breed the horses for competition in horse shows, and for sale.

Oroville: Chinese Temple. This temple, built in 1863, contains several chapels, a courtyard garden, and an assortment of collections.

Pacific Grove: John Steinbeck Memorial Museum. Originally belonging to Steinbeck's grandparents, this house contains memorabilia from the author's youth.

Palm Desert: The Living Desert. The beauty of the world's desert lands is preserved in this 1,200-acre wildlife and botanical park.

Palm Springs: Palm Springs Aerial Tramway. The world's longest double-reversible single span aerial tramway offers spectacular views of the San Jacinto Mountains.

Palo Alto: The Barbie Hall of Fame. This collection contains more than 10,000 Barbie dolls and accessories.

Palomar Mountain: Palomar Observatory. This is the home of the 200-inch Hale telescope, the largest in the United States.

Pasadena: Norton Simon Museum of Art. Works by Monet, Renoir, van Gogh, and Degas are displayed, together with southeast Asian and Indian sculpture.

Petaluma: Winners Circle Ranch. This ranch specializes in the breeding and training of miniature show horses.

Redding: Lake Shasta Caverns. A guided tour includes a boat ride across the McCloud Arm of Lake Shasta.

Riverside: California Museum of Photography. Among the displays are hands-on exhibits which demonstrate how motion pictures are made.

St. Helena: Silverado Museum. This museum contains memorabilia of author Robert Louis Stevenson, including photographs, letters, and original manuscripts.

San Jose: Winchester Mystery House. This 160-room mansion features stairways that go nowhere, trapdoors, and secret passageways.

San Juan Capistrano: Mission San Juan Capistrano. Known for its swallows, which leave each year on October 23rd and return on March 19th, this complex includes the Serra Chapel, which is the oldest building in California.

Sarah L. Winchester began building the Winchester Mystery House in 1884. Having been told by a psychic that she would not die as long as construction on the house continued, Sarah kept adding on to the house haphazardly until her death in 1922.

San Luis Obispo: Mission San Luis Obispo de Tolosa. Built in 1772, this mission still serves as a parish church.

San Marino: Huntington Library, Art Collection and Botanical Gardens. A copy of the Gutenberg Bible is among the rare books contained in this library.

San Mateo: Coyote Point Museum. This modern museum contains hands-on exhibits, dioramas, and a working beehive.

San Pedro: Ports O' Call Village. This recreation of a New England-style village contains 90 shops and restaurants.

San Simeon: Hearst San Simeon

State Historical Monument. The centerpiece of the 137-acre estate of publisher William Randolph Hearst is the magnificent Hearst Castle, surrounded by formal Renaissance gardens.

Santa Barbara: Mission Santa Barbara. Completed in 1820, this example of Spanish Renaissance architecture is one of the best preserved of the missions.

Santa Clara: Great America. This 100-acre theme park

The Mission Santa Barbara was founded in 1786 by Fermin Lasuen, a Franciscan priest. Twice restored after earthquake damage, the mission has not changed its appearance since 1820, and is generally considered the most beautiful in the chain of 21 missions in California.

Visitors on the public tours at Universal Studios get an inside look at the film industry, as well as a closeup view of this movie legend.

consists of five major areas: Hometown Square, Yukon Territory, Yankee Harbor, County Fair, and Orleans Place.

Santa Cruz: The Mystery Spot. The laws of gravity and perspective do not appear to apply in this 150-foot section of redwood forest.

Santa Monica: Angels Attic. This restored Victorian house is devoted to antique dolls, miniatures, and toys.

Santa Rosa: Luther Burbank Home and Gardens. Included in this home of the famed horticulturist is a greenhouse designed by Burbank himself.

Sausalito: Village Fair. Visitors may purchase locally-made handicrafts in specialty shops housed in this three-story building.

Solvang: Old Mission Santa Inés. Founded in 1804, this gold adobe building now contains a museum featuring religious artifacts.

Sonoma: Sonoma State Historic Park. This complex includes the Mission San Francisco Solano and the home of General Mariano Vallejo, founder of Sonoma.

Stockton: Pixie Woods Wonderland. This children's park offers theater programs, as well as rides and an animal petting zoo.

Truckee: Donner Memorial State Park. This 353-acre park is a memorial to the 89-person Donner party, which was stranded in the area by blizzards in the winter of 1846-47.

Universal City: Universal Studios Hollywood. Visitors may tour movie and television sets, and experience live action shows and special effects in California's largest and busiest studio.

Valencia: Six Flags Magic Mountain. This amusement park includes Tidal Wave, Ninja, Freefall, and Viper among its rides.

Vallejo: Marine World Africa USA. This oceanarium and

An orca, also called the killer whale performs at Marine World.

African animal park features more than 1,000 animals in shows and natural settings.

Ventura: San Buenaventura Mission. This was the last mission founded by Father Junípero Serra.

Victorville: Roy Rogers-Dale Evans Museum. This museum contains memorabilia associated with the western film and television stars.

Events

There are many events and organizations that schedule seasonal activities of various kinds in the state of California. Here are some of them.

Sports: Horse racing at Santa Anita Park (Arcadia), MONY Tournament of Champions (Carlsbad), Bidwell Classic Marathon (Chico), Clovis Rodeo (Clovis), World Championship Crab Races and Crab Feed (Crescent City), Gasquet Raft Race (Crescent City), Jumping Frog Jamboree (Del Mar), horse racing at the County Fairgrounds (Del Mar), Blue Angels Golf Tournament (El Centro), Cross-Country Kinetic Sculpture Race (Eureka), White Water Races (Kernville), Kernville Rod Run (Kernville), Great Livermore Airshow (Livermore), Vandenberg AFB Missile Competition and Open House (Lompoc), Toyota Grand Prix (Long Beach), Boat Parades (Long Beach), USA/Mobil Outdoor Track and Field Championships (Los Angeles), Stampede Days (Marysville), West Coast Antique Fly-in (Merced), AT&T Pebble Beach National Pro-Am Golf Championship (Monterey), auto and motorcycle racing at Laguna Seca Raceway (Monterey), skiing at Mt. Shasta Ski Park (Mt. Shasta), Father's Day Bicycle Tour (Nevada City), PRCA Rodeo (Oakdale), Quarter Horse Show (Oakdale), California Dally Team Roping Championships (Oakdale), Tennis Tournament (Ojai), Oxnard Airshow (Oxnard), Bob Hope Chrysler Classic (Palm Desert), Mounted Police Rodeo and Parade (Palm Springs), sled dog races (Palm Springs), Nabisco Dinah Shore Invitational (Palm Springs), World Wrist Wrestling Championships (Petaluma), Red Bluff Roundup (Red Bluff), Red Bluff Boat Drags (Red Bluff), Exchange Club Air Show (Redding), Rodeo Week (Redding), Water Festival (Sacramento), California Rodeo (Salinas), International Airshow (Salinas), Grand National Rodeo, Horse Show and Livestock Exposition (San Francisco), Firefighters Rodeo (San Jose), San Benito County Saddle Horse Show Parade and Rodeo (San Juan Bautista), horse racing at Bay Meadows Racecourse (San Mateo), Summer Sports Festival (Santa Barbara), National Horse and Flower Show (Santa Barbara), Parade of Champions (Santa Clara), Elks Rodeo and Parade (Santa Maria), Sports and Arts Festival (Santa Monica), sled dog races (Truckee), cross-country skiing marathon (Truckee), Truckee-Tahoe Airshow (Truckee), Rodeo (Truckee), Whaleboat Regatta (Vallejo), Whale Watching (Ventura).

Arts and Crafts: Colony Days (Atascadero), Art Festival (Catalina Island), Whole Earth Festival (Davis), Winter Festival (Laguna Beach), Sawdust Festival (Laguna Beach), Fall Festival (Livermore), Cinco de Mayo Celebration (Los Angeles), Old Adobe Fiesta (Petaluma), Children's Lawn Festival (Redding), The Great American Arts Festival (San Jose), Renaissance Faire (San Luis Obispo), Rainbow of Gems and Earth Science Show (Santa Maria), Villa Montalvo Lively Arts Festival (Saratoga), Sausalito Art Festival (Sausalito).

Music: Calico Spring Festival (Barstow), Carmel Bach Festival (Carmel), Russian River Jazz

Festival (Guerneville), Symphony Under the Stars (Hollywood), Long Beach Blues Festival (Long Beach), Long Beach Symphony (Long Beach), Grand Opera (Long Beach), Civic Light Opera and Ballet (Long Beach), Los Angeles Music Center Opera (Los Angeles), Mendocino Festival of Music (Mendocino), Central California Band Review (Merced), Monterey Jazz Festival (Monterey), Ojai Music Festival (Ojai), Oakland Ballet (Oakland), Old Time Fiddlers' Contest (Oroville), Marching Band Festival (Pacific Grove), Shasta Dixieland Jazz Festival (Redding), Dixieland Jazz Festival (Sacramento), Music Circus (Sacramento), Spreckels Outdoor Organ (San Diego), San Francisco Ballet (San Francisco), Midsummer Music Festival (San Francisco), San Francisco Opera (San Francisco), San Francisco Symphony Orchestra (San Francisco), San Jose Symphony (San Jose), Mozart Festival (San Luis Obispo), Cabrillo Music Festival (Santa Cruz), Music at the Vineyards (Saratoga), Jazz on the Waterfront (Stockton).

Entertainment: Fandango Celebration (Alturas), Modoc Last Frontier Fair (Alturas), Contra Costa County Fair (Antioch), Wild West Stampede (Auburn), Gold Panning Show

This happy cook prepares her fare for the Gilroy Garlic Festival.

(Auburn), Placer County Fair (Auburn), Gold Country Fair (Auburn), Museum Heritage Days (Bakersfield), Kern County Fair (Bakersfield), Calico Hullabaloo (Barstow), Calico Spring Festival (Barstow), Calico Days (Barstow), Cherry Festival (Beaumont), Tri-County Fair (Bishop), Colorado River County Fairs (Blythe), Liar's Contest (Borrego Springs), Borrego Days Festival (Borrego Springs), Silverado Days Celebration (Buena Park), Napa County Fair (Calistoga), Pioneer Days (Chico), Silver Dollar Fair (Chico), Expo Fair (Chico), Highland Gathering and Games (Costa Mesa), Orange County Fair (Costa Mesa), Easter in July Lily Festival (Crescent City), Jamboree Days (Crestline), Picnic Day (Davis), Del Mar Fair (Del Mar), Railroad Days (Dunsmuir), Brawley Cattle Call (El Centro), Rhododendron Festival (Eureka), Whale Festival (Fort Bragg), Rhododendron Show (Fort Bragg), Salmon Barbecue (Fort Bragg), Paul Bunyan Days (Fort Bragg), Swedish Festival (Fresno), Obon-Odori Festival (Fresno), Christmas Tree Lane (Fresno), Gilroy Garlic Festival (Gilroy), Nevada County Fair (Grass Valley), Cornish Christmas (Grass Valley), Farmers Fair (Hemet),

Hollywood Christmas Parade (Hollywood), National Date Festival (Indio), Whiskey Flat Days (Kernville), Kernville Stampede (Kernville), Mission San Antonio de Padua Fiesta (King City), Great Sierra Winter Carnival (Lake Tahoe), Wagon Train Caravan (Lake Tahoe), Jeepers Jamboree (Lake Tahoe), Antelope Valley Fair and Alfalfa Festival (Lancaster), Alameda County Fair (Livermore), International Spring Festival (Lodi), Flower Festival (Lompoc), Founding Celebration (Lompoc), Chinese New Year

(Los Angeles), Hanamatsuri (Los Angeles), Asian Cultural Festival (Los Angeles), Nisei Week (Los Angeles), Los Angeles County Fair (Los Angeles), Bok Kai Festival (Marysville), California Prune Festival (Marysville), Mendocino Coast Food and Winefest (Mendocino), Merced County Fair (Merced), Ripon Almond Blossom Festival (Modesto), Graffiti Night (Modesto), Monterey County Fair (Monterey), Spring Fair (Napa), Town and Country Fair (Napa), Constitution Day Parade (Nevada City), Fall Color

A parade of flowers sweeps through the streets of Pasadena to celebrate the annual Rose Bowl.

The inhabitants of Santa Barbara remember the city's Spanish roots with the Old Spanish Days Fiesta and Parade.

Spectacular (Nevada City), Victorian Christmas (Nevada City), Newport Seafest (Newport Beach), Christmas Boat Parade (Newport Beach), Strawberry Festival (Oxnard), Channel Islands Harbor Parade of Lights (Oxnard), Good Ole Days and Victorian Home Tour (Pacific Grove), Wildflower Show (Pacific Grove), Feast of Lanterns (Pacific Grove), Butterfly Parade (Pacific Grove), Tournament of Roses (Pasadena), California Mid-State Fair (Paso Robles), Mission San Miguel Arcángel Fiesta (Paso Robles), Sonoma-Marin Fair (Petaluma), Wagon Train Week (Placerville), El Dorado County Fair (Placerville), Los Angeles County Fair (Pomona), Plumas County Fair (Quincy), Grape Harvest Festival (Rancho Cucamonga), Tehama County Fair (Red Bluff), Shasta District Fair (Redding), San Mateo County Fair and Floral Fiesta (Redwood City), Camellia Festival (Sacramento), California State Fair (Sacramento), National Orange Show (San Bernardino), San Clemente Summer Fiesta (San Clemente), Corpus Christi Fiesta (San Diego), Festival of Bells (San Diego), Admission Day (San Diego), Cabrillo Festival (San Diego), Christmas on the Prado (San Diego), Christmas-Light Boat Parade (San Diego), Blossom Festival (San Diego), Chinese New Year (San Francisco), Cherry Blossom Festival (San Francisco), San Francisco Fair and Exposition (San Francisco), Santa Clara County Fair (San Jose), Early Days Celebration (San Juan Bautista), Festival of Whales (San Juan Capistrano), Fiesta de las Golondrinas (San Juan Capistrano), Adiós a las Golondrinas (San Juan Capistrano), Poly Royal (San Luis Obispo), La Fiesta de San Luis Obispo (San Luis Obispo), Renaissance Faire (San Luis Obispo), San Mateo County Fair and Floral Fiesta (San Mateo), Santa Barbara International Orchid Show (Santa Barbara), Old Spanish Days Fiesta (Santa Barbara), Civil War Reenactment (Santa Cruz), National Begonia Festival (Santa Cruz), Santa Cruz County Fair (Santa Cruz), Santa Barbara County Fair (Santa Maria), Luther Burbank Rose Festival (Santa Rosa), Sonoma County Fair (Santa Rosa), Scottish Gathering and Games (Santa Rosa), Danish Days Festival (Solvang), Valley of the Moon Vintage Festival (Sonoma), Fireman's Muster

(Sonora), Mother Lode Round-Up (Sonora), Mother Lode Fair (Sonora), Stockton Asparagus Festival (Stockton), San Joaquin County Fair (Stockton), Obon Festival and Bazaar (Stockton), Greek Festival (Stockton), Lassen County Fair (Susanville), Conejo Valley Days (Thousand Oaks), Stanislaus County Fair (Turlock), Mendocino County Fair and Apple Show (Ukiah), Solano County Fair (Vallejo), Ventura County Fair (Ventura), Huck

Finn Jubilee (Victorville), San Bernardino County Fair (Victorville).

Tours: Mine tours (Antioch), Catalina tours (Avalon), Eureka's Image Tours (Eureka), Jughandle Ecological Staircase (Fort Bragg), NBC Studios (Burbank), Adobe Tour (Monterey), Victorian Home Tour (Pacific Grove), Gold Bug Mine (Placerville), Naval Ship Tour (San Diego), San Francisco Bay Cruises (San Francisco),

Tour of Old Adobes (San Juan Capistrano), gold prospecting tours (Sonora), agricultural tours (Visalia).

Theater: The Greek Theatre (Berkeley), Lawrence Welk Theater-Museum (Escondido), Ramona Pageant (Hemet), Laguna Moulton Playhouse (Laguna Beach), Greek Theatre in Griffith Park (Los Angeles), Foothill Theatre Company (Nevada City), Woodminster Summer Amphitheater (Oakland), Paramount Theatre (Oakland), Old Globe Theatre (San Diego), Performing Arts Center (San Francisco), American Conservatory Theatre (San Francisco), Shakespeare/Santa Cruz Festival (Santa Cruz), Valley Shakespeare Festival (Saratoga), Solvang Theaterfest (Solvang).

The Old Globe Theatre in San Diego was built in 1935 as a temporary entertainment attraction of the 1935-36 California Pacific International Exposition, but it remained because of its popularity. In 1978 the original building was destroyed by fire, but a new Old Globe Theatre was built and opened in 1982.

Famous People

Many famous people were born in the state of California. Here are a few:

Milton Aborn 1864-1933, Marysville. Impresario

Albert Abrams 1863-1924, San Francisco. Physician and founder of a system of universal diagnosis and treatment of diseases

Bert Acosta 1895-1954, San Diego. Aviator and aeronautical engineer

Annette Adams 1877-1956, Prattville. Attorney and judge

Ansel Adams 1902-84, San Francisco. Photographer

Robert Aitken 1864-1951, Jackson. Astronomer

Gracie Allen 1906-64, San Francisco. Film and television comedienne

Herb Alpert b. 1935, Los Angeles. Grammy Award-winning trumpeter and composer: *A Taste of Honey*

Juan Alvarado 1809-82, Monterey. Governor of Mexican California

Luis Alvarez 1911-88, San Francisco. Nobel Prize-winning physicist

Jack Anderson b. 1922, Long Beach. Pulitzer Prize-winning columnist

Eve Arden 1912-91. Mill Valley. Emmy Award-winning television and film actress: *Our Miss Brooks, Mildred Pierce*

Gertrude Atherton 1857-1948, San Francisco. Author: *The Californians, The Conqueror*

Meredith Baxter-Birney b. 1947, Los Angeles. Television actress: *Family Ties*

Willard Beatty 1891-1961, Berkeley. Educator

David Belasco 1853-1931, San Francisco. Playwright and producer

Candice Bergen b. 1946, Beverly Hills. Film actress: *The Group, Oliver's Story*

Busby Berkeley 1895-1976, Los Angeles. Choreographer and film director

Corbin Bernsen b. 1954, North Hollywood. Television and film actor: *L.A. Law, Major League*

Chuck Berry b. 1926, San Jose. Rock and roll singer and songwriter

Edward Bowes 1874-1946, San Francisco. Conductor of *Major Bowes' Amateur Hour* radio show

Lloyd Bridges b. 1913, San Leandro. Film and television actor: *High Noon, Sea Hunt*

John Brodie b. 1935, San Francisco. Football quarterback

Dave Brubeck b. 1920, Concord. Pianist and composer

Don Budge b. 1915, Oakland. Tennis champion

Leo Buscaglia b. 1924, Los Angeles. Educator and author: *Living, Loving & Learning, The Fall of Freddie the Leaf*

John M. Cage b. 1912, Los Angeles. Composer

Kirk Cameron b. 1970, Panorama City. Television actor: *Growing Pains*

Gary Carter b. 1954, Culver City. Baseball player

Richard Chamberlain b. 1935, Beverly Hills. Film, stage, and television actor: *The Three Musketeers, Dr. Kildare*

Marge Champion b. 1925, Los Angeles. Dancer and

actress

Cher b. 1946, El Centro. Academy Award-winning film actress and singer: *Moonstruck, Mask*

Julia Child b. 1912, Pasadena. Television chef and cookbook author

Maureen Connolly 1934-69, San Diego. Tennis champion

Jackie Cooper b. 1921, Los Angeles. Film actor: *Skippy, The Champ*

William Cooper 1882-1935, Sacramento. U.S. commissioner of education

Harvey Corbett 1873-1954, San Francisco. Architect

James Corbett 1866-1933, San Francisco. First Marquis of Queensberry heavyweight boxing champion

Kevin Costner b. 1955, Los Angeles. Film actor: *Field of Dreams, Dances with Wolves*

Frederick Cottrell 1877-1948, Oakland. Chemist and inventor

Buster Crabbe 1908-83, Oakland. Olympic gold

medal-winning swimmer and film actor

Alan Cranston b. 1914, Palo Alto. Senate leader

Joe Cronin 1906-84, San Francisco. Hall of Fame baseball player and American League president

David Crosby b. 1941, Los Angeles. Rock singer

Ted Danson b. 1947, San Diego. Television and film actor: *Cheers, Three Men and a Baby*

Eric Davis b. 1962, Los Angeles. Baseball player

Glenn Davis b. 1924, Claremont. Football player

Ronald Dellums b. 1935, Oakland. Congressman

Joan Didion b. 1934, Sacramento. Novelist: *Play It as It Lays, A Book of Common Prayer*

Joe DiMaggio b. 1914, Martinez. Hall of Fame baseball player

James Doolittle b. 1896, Alameda. Soldier and airman in World War II

Thomas Dorgan 1877-1929, San Francisco. Cartoonist and sportswriter

Don Drysdale b. 1936, Van Nuys. Hall of Fame baseball pitcher

Robert Duvall b. 1931, San Diego. Academy Award-winning film actor: *Tender Mercies, The Godfather*

Isadora Duncan 1878-1927, San Francisco. Dancer

Clint Eastwood b. 1930, San Francisco. Film actor: *A Fistful of Dollars, Dirty Harry*

Clair Engle 1911-64, Bakersfield. Senate leader

Joseph Erlanger 1874-1965, San Francisco. Nobel Prize-winning physiologist

Nanette Fabray b. 1920, San Diego. Tony Award-winning stage actress: *Love Life*

Mia Farrow b. 1945, Los Angeles. Film actress: *Rosemary's Baby, Hannah and Her Sisters*

Tom Fears b. 1923, Los Angeles. Hall of Fame

football player

Dianne Feinstein b. 1933, San Francisco. Mayor of San Francisco

Sally Field b. 1946, Pasadena. Academy Award-winning film actress: *Norma Rae, Places in the Heart*

Robert Frost 1874-1963, San Francisco. Four-time Pulitzer Prize-winning poet: *New Hampshire, Collected Poems, A Further Range, A Witness Tree*

Frank Gifford b. 1930, Bakersfield. Hall of Fame football player and sports announcer

Sharon Gless b. 1943, Los Angeles. Television actress: *Cagney and Lacey*

Rube Goldberg 1883-1970, San Francisco. Pulitzer Prize-winning cartoonist

Lefty Gomez 1908-89, Rodeo. Hall of Fame baseball pitcher

Pancho Gonzalez b. 1928, Los Angeles. Tennis champion

Gail Goodrich b. 1943, Los Angeles. Basketball player

Farley Granger b. 1925, San Jose. Film actor: *Rope, Strangers on a Train*

Linda Gray b. 1940, Santa Monica. Television actress: *Dallas*

Merv Griffin b. 1925, San Mateo. Entertainer and television producer

Tony Gwynn b. 1960, Los Angeles. Baseball player

Gene Hackman b. 1931, San Bernardino. Film actor: *The French Connection, The Conversation*

Merle Haggard b. 1937, Bakersfield. Country and western singer

Harry Hamlin b. 1951, Pasadena. Television actor: *Studs Lonigan, L.A. Law*

The Hearst San Simeon State Historical Monument was built as a home by William Randolph Hearst, Sr., a wealthy newspaper publisher. At one point in his life, Hearst owned 26 newspapers, 16 magazines, 11 radio stations, 5 news services, and 1 movie company.

Tom Hanks b. 1956, Oakland. Television and film actor: *Bosom Buddies, Big*

Edith Head 1907-81, Los Angeles. Fashion designer

William Randolph Hearst 1863-1951, San Francisco. Publisher

Harry Heilmann 1894-1951, San Francisco. Hall of Fame baseball player

Carla Hills b. 1934, Los Angeles. Lawyer and U.S. secretary of housing and urban development

Dustin Hoffman b. 1937, Los Angeles. Two-time Academy Award-winning film actor: *Kramer vs. Kramer, Rain Man*

Sidney Howard 1891-1939, Oakland. Pulitzer Prize-winning playwright: *They Knew What They Wanted, The Silver Cord*

Timothy Hutton b. 1961, Malibu. Academy Award-winning film actor: *Ordinary People*

Shirley Jackson 1919-65, San Francisco. Novelist and

Jack Kemp, a former New York state congressman and the current secretary of housing and urban development, was the quarterback for the Buffalo Bills of the NFL.

short-story writer: *The Haunting of Hill House,* "The Lottery"

Hiram Johnson 1866-1945, Sacramento. Senate leader

Jack Jones b. 1938, Hollywood. Pop singer

Spike Jones 1911-65, Long Beach. Bandleader

Pauline Kael b. 1919, Petaluma. Film critic

Diane Keaton b. 1946, Los Angeles. Academy Award-winning film actress: *Annie Hall, The Godfather*

Jack Kemp b. 1935, Los Angeles. Football quarterback and U.S. secretary of housing and urban development

Anthony Kennedy b. 1936, Sacramento. Supreme Court justice

Joanna Kerns b. 1953, San Francisco. Television actress: *Growing Pains*

Willis E. Lamb b. 1913, Los Angeles. Nobel Prize-winning physicist

Jesse Lasky 1880-1958, San Jose. Film producer

Vicki Lawrence b. 1949, Inglewood. Emmy Award-winning television actress: *The Carol Burnett Show, Mama's Family*

Ursula LeGuin b. 1929, Berkeley. Novelist: *The Lathe of Heaven, The Dispossessed*

Janet Leigh b. 1927, Merced. Film actress: *Psycho,*

Touch of Evil

Mervyn LeRoy 1900-87, San Francisco. Film director and producer

Malcolm Lockheed 1887-1958, Niles. Aircraft manufacturer and inventor

Jack London 1876-1916, San Francisco. Novelist: *The Call of the Wild, The Sea-Wolf*

Anita Loos 1888-1981, Sissons. Novelist: *Gentlemen Prefer Blondes*

George Lucas b. 1944, Modesto. Film director: *American Graffiti, Star Wars*

Ross Macdonald 1915-83, Los Gatos. Novelist: *The Moving Target, The Barbarous Coast*

Clarence Mackay 1874-1938, San Francisco. Businessman and philanthropist

Judah Magnes 1877-1948, San Francisco. Religious leader and educator

Billy Martin 1928-89, Berkeley. Baseball manager

Tony Martin b. 1913, San Francisco. Pop singer

Stephen Mather 1867-1930, San Francisco. Conservationist

Bob Mathias b. 1930, Tulare. Two-time Olympic gold medal winner in the decathlon

Johnny Mathis b. 1935, San Francisco. Pop singer

Joel McCrea 1905-90, Los Angeles. Film actor: *Foreign Correspondent, Palm Beach Story*

Hugh McElhenny b. 1928, Los Angeles. Hall of Fame football player

Rod McKuen b. 1933, Oakland. Poet and composer: *Listen to the Warm, Lonesome Cities*

Edwin M. McMillan b. 1907, Redondo Beach. Nobel Prize-winning physicist

Liza Minnelli b. 1946, Los Angeles. Academy Award-winning film actress: *Cabaret, The Sterile Cuckoo*

Addison Mizner 1872-1933, Benicia. Architect and real

estate entrepreneur

Marilyn Monroe 1926-62, Los Angeles. Film actress: *How to Marry a Millionaire, Some Like It Hot*

Helen Wills Moody b. 1905, Centerville. Tennis champion

Emma Nevada 1859-1940, near Nevada City. Operatic soprano

Richard Nixon b. 1913, Yorba Linda. Thirty-seventh President of the United States

Isamu Noguchi 1904-88, Los Angeles. Sculptor

Ryan O'Neal b. 1941, Los Angeles. Film actor: *Love Story, Paper Moon*

George S. Patton 1885-1945, near Pasadena. U.S. army general during World War II

Gregory Peck b. 1916, La Jolla. Academy Award-winning film actor: *To Kill a Mockingbird, The Yearling*

Michelle Pfeiffer b. 1957, Santa Ana. Film actress: *Married to the Mob, The*

Fabulous Baker Boys

Bonnie Raitt b. 1949, Burbank. Grammy Award-winning country and western singer: *Nick of Time*

Robert Redford b. 1937, Santa Monica. Film actor: *Butch Cassidy and the Sundance Kid, The Sting*

Sally K. Ride b. 1951, Encino. Astronaut

Robert Ripley 1893-1949, Santa Rosa. Newspaper feature artist, creator of *Ripley's Believe It or Not*

John Ritter b. 1948, Burbank. Emmy Award-winning television actor: *Three's Company*

Cliff Robertson b. 1925, La Jolla. Academy Award-winning film actor: *Charly, PT-109*

Josiah Royce 1855-1916, Grass Valley. Idealist philosopher

Pete Rozelle b. 1926, South Gate. Football commissioner

William Saroyan 1908-81, Fresno. Pulitzer Prize-winning playwright and novelist: *The Time of Your Life, The Human Comedy*

Robert P. Scripps 1895-1938, San Diego. Newspaper publisher

Tom Seaver b. 1944, Fresno. Baseball pitcher

Zoot Sims 1925-85, Inglewood. Saxophonist

O. J. Simpson b. 1947, San

Duke Snider was playing with the Brooklyn Dodgers when the team moved to Los Angeles, the city of his birth.

Francisco. Hall of Fame football player

Duke Snider b. 1926, Los Angeles. Hall of Fame baseball player

Suzanne Somers b. 1946, San Bruno. Television actress: *Three's Company*

Robert Stack b. 1919, Los Angeles. Emmy Award-winning television and film actor: *The Untouchables, The High and the Mighty*

Lincoln Steffens 1866-1936, San Francisco. Journalist and political reformer

John Steinbeck 1902-68, Pulitzer and Nobel Prize-winning author: *The Grapes of Wrath, Of Mice and Men*

Adlai E. Stevenson 1900-65, Los Angeles. Politician and government official

Irving Stone 1903-89 San Francisco. Novelist: *Lust for Life, The Agony and the Ecstasy*

Darryl Strawberry b. 1962, Los Angeles. Baseball player

Lynn Swann b. 1952, Foster City. Hall of Fame football player

Shirley Temple b. 1928, Santa Monica. Child film actress and U.S. ambassador

Gwen Verdon b. 1925, Los Angeles. Two-time Tony Award-winning stage actress, dancer, and singer: *Damn Yankees, Redhead*

Bill Walton b. 1952, La Mesa. Basketball player

Earl Warren 1891-1974, Los Angeles. Chief Justice of the Supreme Court

Ted Williams b. 1939, San Diego. Hall of Fame baseball player

Paul Winfield b. 1941, Los Angeles. Television actor: *Julia, Roots: The Next Generation*

Colleges and Universities
There are many colleges and universities in California. Here are the more prominent, with their locations, dates of founding, and enrollments.

Academy of Art College, San Francisco, 1929, 2,153

Art Center College of Design, Pasadena, 1930, 1,185

Azusa Pacific University, Azusa, 1899, 2,933

Biola University, La Mirada, 1908, 2,566

California College of Arts and Crafts, Oakland, 1907, 1,058

California Institute of Technology, Pasadena, 1891, 1,841

California Lutheran College, Thousand Oaks, 1959, 2,853

California Polytechnic State University, San Luis Obispo, San Luis Obispo, 1901, 17,564

California State Polytechnic University, Pomona, Pomona, 1938, 19,579

California State University, Bakersfield, Bakersfield, 1965, 5,215; *Chico*, Chico, 1887, 16,569; *Dominguez Hills*, Carson, 1960, 8,819; *Fresno*, Fresno, 1911, 19,124; *Fullerton*, Fullerton, 1957, 24,961;

Hayward, Hayward, 1957, 12,825; *Long Beach*, Long Beach, 1949, 32,875; *Los Angeles*, Los Angeles, 1947, 20,804; *Northridge*, Northridge, 1958, 30,657; *Sacramento*, Sacramento, 1947, 25,559; *San Bernardino*, San Bernardino, 1960, 10,873

Chapman College, Orange, 1861, 2,221

College of Notre Dame, Belmont, 1851, 1,066

DeVry Institute of Technology, City of Industry, 1983, 1,965

Fresno Pacific College, Fresno, 1944, 1,364

Golden Gate University, San Francisco, 1901, 8,729

Humboldt State University, Arcata, 1913, 7,301

Loma Linda University, Loma Linda, 1905, 4,243

Los Angeles College of Chiropractic, Whittier, 1911, 1,003

Loyola Marymount University, Los Angeles, 1865, 5,347

Master's College, Newhall, 1927, 1,008

Mills College, Oakland, 1852, 1,050

Mount St. Mary's College, Los Angeles, 1925, 1,152

National University, San Diego, 1971, 10,318

Northrop University, Inglewood, 1942, 1,057

Occidental College, Los Angeles, 1887, 1,697

Pacific Union College, Angwin, 1882, 1,678

Pepperdine University, Malibu, 1937, 3,816;

Point Loma College, San Diego, 1902, 2,221

Pomona College, Claremont, 1887, 1,390

Saint Mary's College of California, Moraga, 1863, 3,605

San Diego State University, San Diego, 1897, 35,582

San Francisco State University, San Francisco, 1899, 28,120

San Jose State University, San Jose, 1857, 29,847

Santa Clara University, Santa Clara, 1851, 7,892

Sonoma State University, Rohnert Park, 1960, 8,759

Stanford University, Stanford, 1885, 13,354

United States International University, San Diego, 1952, 3,530

University of California at Berkeley, Berkeley, 1868, 31,612; *Davis*, Davis, 1906, 22,571; *Irvine*, Irvine, 1965, 16,149; *Los Angeles*, Los Angeles, 1919, 36,378; *Riverside*, Riverside, 1954, 8,220; *San Diego*, La Jolla, 1959, 17,595; *Santa Barbara*, Santa Barbara, 1891, 19,082; *Santa Cruz*, Santa Cruz, 1965, 9,784

University of La Verne, La Verne, 1891, 5,933

University of Redlands, Redlands, 1907, 2,300

University of San Diego, San Diego, 1949, 5,921

University of San Francisco, San Francisco, 1855, 6,028

University of Southern California, Los Angeles, 1880, 29,021

University of the Pacific, Stockton, 1851, 5,800

West Coast University, Los Angeles, 1909, 1,600

Western State University College of Law of Orange County, Fullerton, 1966, 1,340

Westmont College, Santa Barbara, 1940, 1,256

Whittier College, Whittier, 1901, 1,579

Where To Get More Information
California Office of Tourism
P.O. Box 9278, T98, Dept. 1003
Van Nuys, CA 91409
Or Call 1-800-862-2543

Hawaii

The state seal of Hawaii, adopted in 1959, has a shield in the center. To the left stands Kamehameha I, and to the right the Goddess of Liberty holding the Hawaiian flag in her right hand. The sun rises behind the shield and "1959" appears above it. At the bottom is the Phoenix surrounded by taro leaves, banana foliage, and sprays of maidenhair fern. The state motto and "State of Hawaii" are printed in the outer circle of the seal. When color is added, it becomes the state coat of arms.

State Flag

The state flag of Hawaii consists of alternating white, red, and blue stripes representing the eight main islands. The upper left corner contains the Union Jack of Great Britain.

State Motto

Ua mau ke ea o ka aina i ka pono
The translation of the Hawaiian motto is "The life of the land is perpetuated in righteousness." These words were spoken by King Kamehameha III in 1843.

The natural beauty of the Hawaii islands is accented by a rainbow arching over Wailua Falls.

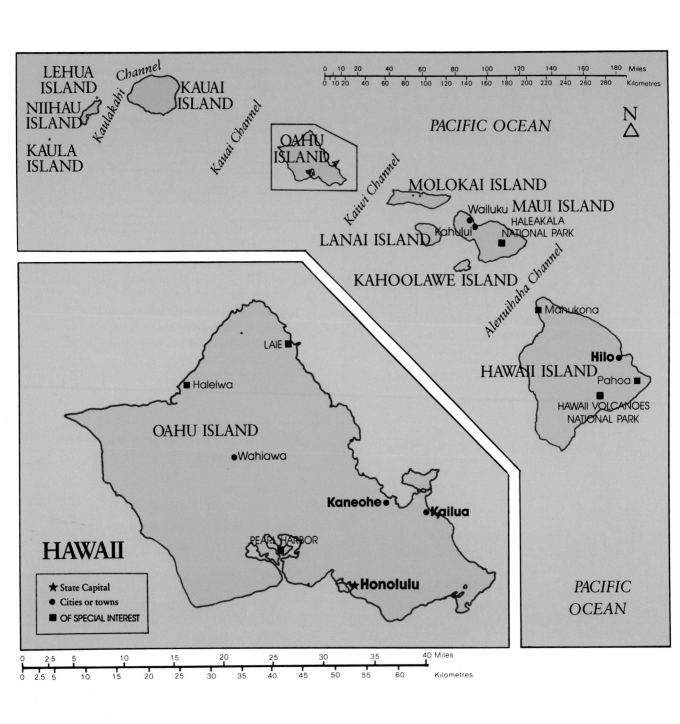

State Capital

Honolulu has been the official capital of the islands since 1845. Upon Hawaii's admission to the Union in 1959, the city continued as state capital. In 1965, construction began on the capitol building. When it was dedicated in 1969, the total cost, including furnishings, came to $24,576,900. Built of steel and concrete, the structure stands in the center of an 80,000-square-foot reflecting pool, symbolizing the birth of the islands from the ocean. The legislative chamber is in the shape of a truncated dome, resembling a volcano, likewise representing the creation of the islands. The building is surrounded by forty columns shaped like royal palms.

The State Capitol of Hawaii is one of the few official buildings in Honolulu that does not have any connections to the old monarchy.

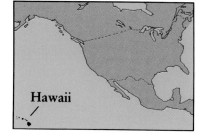

State Name and Nicknames

The origin of the state name is not known. It may have come from Hawaii Loa, the traditional discoverer of islands, or from Hawaiki, the traditional Polynesian homeland. "Hawaii" is a combination of two words: *Hawa*, meaning "traditional homeland," and *ii*, meaning "small" or "raging," which may refer to Hawaii's volcanoes.

Since 1959, Hawaii has been officially known as the *Aloha State*. Other nicknames include *Paradise of the Pacific* for its natural beauty, the *Pineapple State* for its pineapple industry, and the *Youngest State* because it was the last state to join the Union.

In addition to the state nicknames, seven of the eight main islands have their own unofficial nicknames. Hawaii is known as the *Big Island* because it is the largest in the chain. Maui, the *Valley Island*, has many canyons dominating its landscape. Molokai is called the *Friendly Island* for the courtesy shown to visitors by its inhabitants. Since Lanai is owned by the Dole Company, it is often referred to as the *Pineapple Island*. The *Gathering Place* is the nickname of Oahu, the center of Hawaiian life for nearly 80 percent of the state's residents, and millions of tourists who visit each year. The lush greenery and spectacular beauty of Kauai give rise to its nickname, the *Garden Island*.

The Hawaiian goose has evolved to suit its lava-filled environment by developing claw-like feet and a wing structure better suited for short flights.

The Pua Aloalo is the official flower for the state of Hawaii.

Niihau, the *Forbidden Island*, is privately owned. It is inaccessible to visitors without the owners' permission.

State Fish

The *humuhumunukunuku-a-pua'a*, or rectangular triggerfish, has been the state fish since 1985.

State Tree

The kukui, also known as candlenut, *Aleurites moluccana*, was named state tree in 1959.

State Bird

The nene, or Hawaiian goose, *Nesochen sandwicensis* or *Bernicata sandwicensis*, was designated state bird in 1957.

State Flower

In 1923, Pua Aloalo, or yellow Hibiscus Brackenridgei, was selected official flower. In addition to the state flower, each of the islands has an official flower: Red Lehua, or Ohia (Hawaii); Lokelani, or Pink Cottage Rose (Maui); White Kukui Blossom (Molokai); Hinahina, or Beach Heliotrope (Kahoolawe); Kaunaoa, or Yellow and Orange Air Plant (Lanai); Ilima (Oahu); Mokihana, or Green Berry (Kauai); and, White Pupu Shell (Niihau).

State Languages

Although many others are spoken in the islands, Hawaii's official languages are English and Hawaiian. There are only 12 letters in the Hawaiian alphabet: *a, e, i, o, u, h, k, l, m, n, p,* and *w*. It is one of the world's most musical tongues.

State Marine Mammal

In 1979, the humpback whale was named Hawaii's state marine mammal.

State Song

"Hawaii Ponoi," with words by King Kalakaua and music by Henry Berger, was adopted as state song in 1967. It means "Hawaii's own."

Population

The population of Hawaii in 1990 was 1,115,274, making it the 40th most populous state. There are 172.3 persons per square mile—54 percent of the population live in towns and cities. Although about 86 percent of the people were born in the United States, only about 12 percent are of mostly Hawaiian ancestry. Other ethnic groups include the Japanese, Filipinos, Chinese, Koreans, Hispanics, and Samoans.

Geography and Climate

Hawaii, an archipelago made up of 132 islands, is located in the Pacific Ocean,

The sight of a whale frolicking in the ocean is not uncommon for the island inhabitants of Hawaii.

Smoke rises out of Kilauea Crater, one of the many volcanoes that helped form the Hawaii islands.

2,397 miles southwest of San Francisco. The only state not located on the North American continent, it has an area of 6,471 square miles, making it the 47th largest state. Only seven of the eight main islands are inhabited. Kahoolawe, the smallest of these, is used by the U.S. military for target practice. The remaining 124 islands have a combined area of only 3 square miles. The climate of the state is subtropical, with wide variations in rainfall. Waialeale, on the island of Kauai, is the wettest spot in the United States, averaging 444 inches of rain per year.

The islands are actually the tops of submerged volcanic mountains formed hundreds of thousands of years ago. Mauna Loa and Kilauea are active volcanoes located on the "Big Island" of Hawaii. The highest point in the state, at 13,796 feet, is Mauna Kea, a dormant volcano in Hawaii County, while the lowest point is at sea level along the coast. Major waterways in the state are the Anahulu, Halawa, Kamananui, Kaukonahua, Poamoho, Waiawa, Wailuku, and Waimea rivers. There are very few lakes in the state. Salt Lake on Oahu, and Halalii Lake and Halulu Lake on Niihau, are the most significant.

Industries

The principal industries of the state are tourism, sugar refining, pineapples and diversified agriculture, aquaculture, fishing, motion pictures, scientific research, and publishing. The chief manufactured products are sugar, canned pineapple, clothing, processed foods, and printing.

Agriculture

The chief crops of Hawaii are sugar, pineapple, macadamia nuts, fruits, coffee, vegetables, melons, and floriculture, especially orchids. Hawaii is also a livestock state. There are estimated to be some 208,000 cattle and calves, 43,000 hogs and pigs, and 1.22 million chickens on its farms. Crushed stone and cement are important mineral products, and commercial fishing brings in approximately $47.1 million per year.

Government

The governor and lieutenant governor are elected for four-year terms. Other top officials, including the attorney general, comptroller, and finance director, are appointed by the governor with the approval of the senate. The state legislature, which meets annually, consists of 25 senators and 51 representatives. The senators are elected from 25 senatorial districts for four-year terms; the representatives are elected from 51 representative districts for two-year terms. The present constitution, which took effect in 1959, was originally approved in 1950 when Hawaii was still a territory. It was modified in 1968 and 1978, and by 1984, seventy-five amendments had been added to the document. In addition to its two U.S. senators, Hawaii has two representatives in the U.S. House of Representatives and four votes in the electoral college.

History

About 2,000 years ago, the Polynesians arrived in Hawaii. They came from other Pacific islands, sailing across the ocean in giant double-hulled canoes.

Captain James Cook was the first white man to step on the Hawaiian Islands, arriving in Waimea, Kauai on January 19, 1778.

Around A.D. 1200, the Tahitians, another group of Polynesians, came to Hawaii and gained control over the earlier settlers.

In 1778, Captain James Cook of the British Royal Navy sighted Oahu and landed on Kauai, naming the archipelago the Sandwich Islands, after the Earl of Sandwich. At the time, local chiefs ruled each island independently. In 1782, Kamehameha came to the throne of one of the kingdoms and began a campaign to unite the islands. Aided by firearms obtained from white traders, he succeeded in gaining control of all but two of the islands by 1795. Kauai and Niihau joined the Kingdom of Hawaii in 1810.

Trading ships visiting Hawaii often brought diseases from other parts of the world. A cholera epidemic killed many people in 1804. The sandalwood trade with China, which developed during the early

1800s, provided a great source of income for the islands.

When Kamehameha II took the throne following his father's death in 1819, he did away with the Hawaiian religion, which included among its rites human sacrifice and idol worship. Hiram Bingham, a Protestant missionary, and his followers arrived in Hawaii the next year and converted most of the natives to Christianity. In 1827, Roman Catholic missionaries tried to bring Catholicism to the region. Because many Hawaiian chiefs considered Protestantism the official religion, the missionaries met with much resistance and were forced to leave in 1831. Roman Catholics were given religious freedom and, after 1840, their number grew.

During that same year, Hawaii's first constitution was adopted. It provided for a legislative body consisting of a council of chiefs, and representatives elected by the

Kamehameha I is thought to have been born in 1758, on the Kohala peninsula on the Hawaii island. He succeeded in unifying most of the islands in 1796, establishing a dynasty that would last for almost one hundred years.

people. In 1842, the United States recognized Hawaii as an independent government and, shortly thereafter, France and Great Britain did the same.

The sugar industry began to develop during the 1850s. Because of the need for more workers, the sugarcane growers brought many Chinese to the islands. People from other parts of the world began to arrive: Japanese and Portuguese around 1870; Filipinos, Koreans, and Puerto Ricans around 1900.

In 1874, David Kalakaua was elected king by the legislature. It was during his reign that a treaty was negotiated giving the United States exclusive use of Pearl Harbor as a naval station and securing a market for Hawaiian sugar. When Kalakaua died in 1891, he was succeeded by his sister, Liliuokalani. She tried to restore some of the power of the monarchy, but was ousted in 1893 during a bloodless revolution. A new government was established and Sanford B. Dole became the first, and only, president of the Republic of Hawaii.

In 1898, Hawaii's important military location was recognized, and the islands were annexed by the United States. Hawaii achieved territorial status in 1900. It was during this time that James B. Dole, a cousin of Sanford B. Dole, succeeded in producing canned pineapple. This was the beginning of what was to become Hawaii's second major industry.

Military installations were built by the United States Navy and Army shortly before World War I, and many Hawaiians participated in the war. Because of the continuing U. S. military buildup, the Great Depression of the 1930s was not felt as deeply in Hawaii as in the rest of the nation.

On December 7, 1941, the Japanese navy attacked Pearl Harbor by air, causing much loss of life and damage to the U.S. military, and plunging the United States into World War II. At the start of the war, some Americans feared disloyalty from Hawaiians of Japanese descent. However, their fears were unfounded;

Many members of the 442nd Regimental Combat Team, consisting mainly of Japanese-Americans, fought bravely in Italy and France.

Beginning in 1919, several bills for Hawaiian statehood were brought before Congress. These failed to pass because many congressmen were still afraid that the large Oriental population might not be loyal to the United States in a war. In 1950, Hawaiians approved the constitution that would take effect upon the territory's admission to the Union. Finally, in 1959, Hawaii became the 50th state.

Today, Hawaii's population has increased and its economy has boomed. Tourism has become its third major industry, with new resort areas opening on the islands of Hawaii, Kauai, Maui, and Molokai.

Sports

Hawaii is a state involved in many sports and activities. On the collegiate level, football's Aloha Bowl is

This view of the Honolulu skyline shows that the state is not composed entirely of beaches.

played each year in Honolulu's Aloha Stadium, as is the Hula Bowl. On the professional level, the National Football League Pro Bowl Game, matching the National Football Conference and American Football Conference all-stars, is also played in Aloha Stadium.

Major Cities

Hilo (population 35,300). The heritage of the "Big Island's" capital city is mostly Japanese. Surrounded by sugarcane plantations and orchards, it is the center of the state's thriving orchid industry.

Things to see in Hilo: Akaka Falls State Park, Hawaiian Tropical Botanical Garden, Kaumana Caves, Liliuokalani Gardens Park, Lyman Mission House and Museum, Mauna Kea State Park, Mauna Loa Macadamia Nut Plant, Nani Mau Gardens, and Rainbow Falls.

Honolulu (population 376,110). Discovered in 1794 when Captain William Brown of England entered what is now Honolulu Harbor, the capital city is known as the "Crossroads of the Pacific." The thriving modern metropolis, with its high-rise hotels and condominiums, still retains its ancient exotic charm.

Places to visit in Honolulu: Bishop Museum, Contemporary Museum, Dole Cannery Square, Foster Botanic Garden, Hawaii Maritime Center, Honolulu Academy of Arts, Iolani Palace State Monument, Kamehameha Schools, Kawaiahao Church, King Kamehameha's Statue, Lyon Arboretum, Mission Houses Museum, Neal S. Blaisdell Center, Nuuanu Pali State Wayside, Our Lady of Peace Cathedral, Paradise Park, Punahou School, Queen Emma Summer Palace, State Capitol, Diamond Head State Monument, Honolulu Zoo, Queen Kapiolani Hibiscus Garden, Waikiki Aquarium, Royal Gallery, and the U.S. Army Museum of Hawaii.

Occasionally a volcano on Hawaii erupts with angry abandon as Puu O'o in Hawaii does in this picture.

Places To Visit

The National Park Service maintains 7 areas in the state of Hawaii: Haleakala National Park, Hawaii Volcanoes National Park, Kalaupapa National Historical Park, Kaloko-Honokohau National Historical Park, Puuhonua o Honaunau National Historical Park, Puukohola Heiau National Historic Site, and the USS *Arizona* Memorial. In addition, there are 23 state recreation areas.

Haleiwa (Oahu): Waimea Falls Park. This 1,800-acre park

features an arboretum, botanical garden, diving shows, and hula performances.

Hana (Maui): Waianapanapa State Park and Cave. The water in this cave periodically turns red because of numerous tiny red shrimp. But, according to legend, it is caused by the blood of a murdered Hawaiian princess.

Hanalei (Kauai): Waioli Mission House. This two-story house, built by Reverend William P. Alexander, was one of the first American-style homes on the island.

Honaunau (Hawaii): The Painted Church. The first Catholic church on the island contains elaborate murals depicting scenes from Biblical history.

Kaanapali (Maui): Whaler's Village Museum. A complete skeleton of a sperm whale is the centerpiece of this museum.

Kailua Kona (Hawaii): Atlantis Submarines. Underwater voyages allow visitors to explore the variety of life found in the area.

Kalaheo (Kauai): Olu Pua Botanical Gardens. A plantation house built in 1931 stands in the center of twelve-and-a-half acres of gardens filled with exotic plants and palm trees.

Kaneohe (Oahu): Byodo-In Temple. This replica of a 900-year-old Japanese temple is set beneath the cliffs of the Koolau Mountains.

Kilauea (Kauai): St. Sylvester's Roman Catholic Church. This octagonal church, constructed of lava rock and wood, contains frescoes by Jean Charlot.

Koloa (Kauai): Spouting Horn. A geyser-like effect is formed as wave action forces water through a hole in a lava formation.

Lahaina (Maui): The Wo Hing Temple and Museum. Built in 1912, this restored building contains rare Chinese artifacts.

Laie (Oahu): Polynesian Cultural Center. This 35-acre re-creation of a group of South Seas island villages allows visitors to sample a variety of cultures.

Lanai City (Lanai): Garden of the Gods. This assortment of odd geologic formations, caused by erosion, changes color with the setting sun.

A whale skeleton is prominently exhibited in this whaler's village on Lahaina, Maui.

Lihue (Kauai): Kauai Museum. The history of Kauai, "The Garden Isle," is explored in this two-building complex.

Mahukona (Hawaii): Lapakahi State Historical Park. The remains of houses and canoe sheds can be seen in this 600-year-old Hawaiian settlement, which has been recently excavated.

Maunaloa (Molokai): Molokai Ranch Wildlife Park. This 800-acre preserve is home to 400 species of African and Asian animals.

Napoopoo (Hawaii): Captain Cook Memorial. The memorial, a submerged plaque accessible only by boat, marks the spot where

The Fern Grotto on Kauai island.

Captain James Cook was killed.

Pahala (Hawaii): Punaluu Black Sand Beach Park. The gleaming black sand of the beach was formed when boiling lava poured into the ocean.

Pahoa (Hawaii): Lava Tree State Monument. These tree molds were formed in 1790 when molten lava swept through a grove of ohia trees.

Wailua (Kauai): Fern Grotto. A one-and-a-half-hour boat ride on the Wailua River brings visitors to this beautiful fern-festooned cave, which is a popular site for weddings.

Wailuku (Maui): Maui Historical Society Museum. This museum houses ancient Hawaiian artifacts, and paintings by Edward Bailey.

Waimanalo Beach (Oahu): Sea Life Park. This 62-acre oceanarium offers numerous shows, exhibits, and lectures.

Waimea (Hawaii): Kamuela Museum. This extensive collection of early Hawaiian artifacts includes pieces from the Iolani Palace in Honolulu.

Waimea (Kauai): Waimea Canyon State Park. This 10-mile series of brilliantly colored gorges cut into the Alakai Plateau is inhabited by wild goats.

Polo matches at the Hawaii Polo Club.

Events

There are many events and organizations that schedule seasonal activities of various kinds in the state of Hawaii. Here are some of them.

Sports: Kilauea Volcano Wilderness Marathon and Rim Runs (Hawaii Volcanoes National Park, Hawaii), Keiki Fishing Tournament (Kailua-Kona, Hawaii), Bud Light Ironman Triathlon World Championships (Hawaii), Pele's Cup (Mauna Lao, Hawaii), Big Island Ultraman National Championship (Kailua-Kona, Hawaii), Parker Ranch Rodeo and Horse Races (Waimea, Hawaii), Hawaii International Billfish Tournament (Kailua-Kona, Hawaii), Archer's Invitational Tournament and Black Deer Hunt (Waimea, Kauai), Hepthalon Fitness Celebration (Poipu Beach, Kauai), Hanalei Stampede (Hanalei, Kauai), Haleakala Run to the Sun (Kahului, Maui), Maui Classic (Lahaina, Maui), LPGA Women's Kemper Open Golf Tournament (Wailea, Maui), Makawao Statewide Rodeo (Maui), Molokai-to-Oahu Outrigger Canoe Race

The Waikiki Shell is a famous outdoor stage on the island of Oahu.

(Maunaloa, Molokai), Triple Crown of Surfing (Oahu), Honolulu Marathon (Honolulu, Oahu), auto racing at Hawaii Raceway Park (Honolulu, Oahu), Outrigger Hotel Top Gun Hydrofest/Pearl Harbor Aloha Festival (Pearl Harbor, Oahu), International Boogie Bodyboard Championships (Oahu), Hawaii Formula 40 World Cup (Honolulu, Oahu), Rainbow Classic (Honolulu, Oahu), Hawaiian Open Golf Tournament (Honolulu, Oahu), Buffalo's Annual Big Board Surfing Classic (Oahu), polo matches at the Hawaii Polo Club (Mokuleia, Oahu), Wahine Bodyboard Championships (Sandy Beach, Oahu), Pro Surf

Aloha Week, held every year in September, features dancing and craft demonstrations.

Championships (Sandy Beach, Oahu), Waikiki Rough Water Swim (Oahu).

Arts and Crafts: Hilo Orchid Society Show (Hilo, Hawaii), Big Island Bonsai Show (Hilo, Hawaii), Hawaii State Horticultural Show (Hilo, Hawaii), Establishment Day Cultural Festival (Kawaihae, Hawaii), Coco Palms Summer Crafts Festival (Wailua, Kauai), Art Maui (Makawao, Maui), Mission Houses Museum Annual Christmas Fair (Honolulu, Oahu), Downtown Christmas Crafts Fair (Honolulu, Oahu), Honolulu Academy of Arts (Honolulu, Oahu), Okinawan Festival (Honolulu, Oahu), Fancy Fair (Honolulu, Oahu), Pacific Handcrafters Guild Fair (Honolulu, Oahu), Sandcastle Building Contest (Oahu), Orchid Show (Honolulu, Oahu).

Music: Karaoke Festival (Hilo, Hawaii), King Kalakaua Kupuna and Keiki Hula Festival (Hawaii), Kapalua Music Festival (Maui), Prince Lot Hula Festival (Oahu), Ukulele Festival (Honolulu, Oahu), Ka Himeni Ana (Honolulu, Oahu), Kanikapila (Honolulu, Oahu), Gabby Pahinui/Atta Isaacs Slack-Key Guitar Fest (Honolulu, Oahu), Queen Liliuokalani Keiki Hula Competition (Oahu), Honolulu Symphony Orchestra (Honolulu, Oahu), Hawaii Opera Theatre (Honolulu, Oahu).

Entertainment: Lei Day (all islands), Bon Odori Festivals (all Islands), Aloha Week Festivals (all islands), Kona Coffee Festival (Kailua-Kona, Hawaii), Kona Nightingale Race (Kailua-Kona, Hawaii), Almost Golden Lobster Hunt (Kailua-Kona, Hawaii), International Festival of the Pacific (Hilo, Hawaii), Merrie Monarch Festival (Hilo, Hawaii), Establishment Day (Kawaihae, Hawaii), Captain Cook Festival (Waimea, Kauai), Ke Ola Hou Hawaiian Spring Festival (Hanapepe, Kauai), Koloa Plantation Days (Koloa Town, Kauai), Na Mele O'Maui Festival (Lahaina, Maui), Maui Jaycees Carnival (Maui), Barrio Festival (Wailuku, Maui), Pearl Harbor Aloha Festival (Pearl Harbor, Oahu), Festival of the Pacific (Honolulu, Oahu), Hawaii State Fair (Honolulu, Oahu), Hawaii Mardi Gras (Honolulu, Oahu), East-West Center International Fair (Honolulu, Oahu), The Great Hawaiian Rubber Duckie Race (Honolulu, Oahu), Compadres South Pacific Chili Exposition Cookoff (Honolulu,

Oahu), Hawaii State Farm Fair (Oahu), Carole Kai International Bed Race and Parade (Waikiki, Oahu), Hawaii Challenge National Sport Kite Festival and Annual Oahu Kite Festival (Waikiki, Oahu), Kodak Hula Show (Waikiki, Oahu), Christmas Parade (Honolulu, Oahu), Narcissus Festival (Honolulu, Oahu), Punahou Carnival (Oahu), Cherry Blossom Festival (Honolulu, Oahu), Hula Festival (Honolulu, Oahu), The Japan Festival (Honolulu, Oahu), Makahiki Festival (Haleiwa, Oahu), The Young People's Hula Show (Honolulu, Oahu).

Tours: Waipi'o Valley Shuttle and Tours (Kukuihaele, Hawaii), Fern Grotto (Wailua, Kauai), Molokai Mule Ride (Kalaupapa National Historical Park, Molokai), Pony Express Tours (Haleakala National Park, Maui), Blue Hawaiian Helicopters (Kahului, Maui), Lahaina-Kaanapali & Pacific Railroad (Lahaina, Maui), Dole Cannery Square (Honolulu, Oahu), Chinatown Tours (Honolulu, Oahu), Glider Rides (Mokuleia, Oahu), Pearl Harbor Cruises (Pearl Harbor, Oahu).

Theater: Maui Community Arts and Cultural Center (Kahului, Maui), Hawaii International Film Festival (Oahu), John F. Kennedy Theatre (Honolulu, Oahu),

Manoa Valley Theatre (Honolulu, Oahu), Ruger Theatre (Honolulu, Oahu).

Famous People

Many famous people were born in the state of Hawaii. Here are a few:

William D. Alexander 1833-1913, Honolulu, Oahu. Historian and scientist

Samuel Armstrong 1839-93, Maui. Educator

Henry Baldwin 1842-1911, Lahaina, Oahu. Sugar grower and capitalist

Hiram Bingham 1831-1908, Honolulu, Oahu. Missionary to Micronesia

Henry Carter 1837-91, Honolulu, Oahu. Merchant and diplomat

William Castle 1878-1963. Honolulu, Oahu. Diplomat and author

Ron Darling b. 1960, Honolulu, Oahu. Baseball pitcher

Walter Dillingham 1875-1963, Honolulu, Oahu. Business executive

Sanford Dole 1844-1926, Honolulu, Oahu. President of the Republic of Hawaii and governor of the Territory of Hawaii

Sid Fernandez b. 1962, Honolulu, Oahu. Baseball pitcher

Erin Gray b. 1952, Honolulu, Oahu. Television actress: *Buck Rogers in the 25th Century, Silver Spoons*

John Gulick 1832-1923, Waimea, Kauai. Missionary, naturalist, and writer on evolution

Luther Gulick 1865-1918, Honolulu, Oahu. Educator

William Hillebrand 1853-1925, Honolulu, Oahu. Chemist

Don Ho b. 1930, Kakaako, Oahu. Singer and entertainer

Charlie Hough b. 1948, Honolulu, Oahu. Baseball pitcher

Daniel K. Inouye b. 1924, Honolulu, Oahu. Congressman

Duke Kahanamoku 1890-

1968, near Waikaiki, Oahu. Three-time Olympic gold medal-winning swimmer

Jonah Kalanianaole 1871-1922, Kauai. Delegate to Congress from Hawaii

Kamehameha I 1758-1819, Kohala district, Hawaii. Founder and first monarch of unified Hawaii

Jesse Kuhaulua b. 1944, Hawaii. Champion sumo wrestler

George Lathrop 1851-98, near Honolulu, Oahu. Author and editor: *Rose and Rooftree, Spanish Vistas*

Queen Liliuokalani 1838-1917, Honolulu, Oahu. Last monarch of the Hawaiian Islands

Mike Lum b. 1945, Honolulu, Oahu. Baseball player

Ellison Onizuka 1946-86, Kealakekua, Kona, Hawaii. Astronaut

Poncie Ponce b. 1933, Maui. Television actor: *Hawaiian Eye*

Red Rocha b. 1923, Hilo, Hawaii. Basketball player

Don Stroud b. 1937, Honolulu, Oahu. Television actor: *Mickey Spillane's Mike Hammer*

Lorrin Thurston 1858-1931, Honolulu, Oahu. Lawyer and editor

Milt Wilcox b. 1950, Honolulu, Oahu. Baseball pitcher

Colleges and Universities

There are several colleges and universities in Hawaii. Here are the most prominent, with their locations, dates of founding, and enrollments.

Brigham Young University—Hawaii Campus, Laie, Oahu, 1955, 2,040

Chaminade University of Honolulu, Honolulu, Oahu, 1955, 2,610

Hawaii Pacific College, Honolulu, Oahu, 1965, 4,962

University of Hawaii at Manoa, Honolulu, Oahu 1907, 18,622

Ellison Onizuka, the first Japanese-American astronaut, was on board the spaceship Challenger *on the day of its tragic accident.*

Where To Get More Information

Hawaii Visitors Bureau
2270 Kalakaua Avenue
Honolulu, HI 96815
Or Call 1-808-923-1811

Bibliography

General

Aylesworth, Thomas G. and Virginia L. Aylesworth. *Let's Discover the States: The Pacific.* New York: Chelsea House, 1988.

California

Bean, Walton. *California: An Interpretive History,* 3rd ed. New York: McGraw Hill, 1978.

Beck, Warren A., and Williams, D. A. *California: A History of the Golden State.* New York: Doubleday, 1972.

Buff, Mary and Conrad. *Big Tree.* New York: Viking, 1946.

Carpenter, Allan. *California,* rev. ed. Chicago: Childrens Press, 1978.

Caughey, John W. *California: A Remarkable State's Life History,* 3rd ed. Englewood Cliffs, NJ: Prentice-Hall, 1970.

Curry, Jane L. *Down from the Lonely Mountain: California Indian Tales.* New York: Harcourt, 1965.

Fradin, Dennis B. *California in Words and Pictures.* Chicago: Childrens Press, 1977.

Johnson, William W. *The Forty-Niners.* New York: Time Inc., 1974.

Lavender, David S. *California: Land of New Beginnings.* New York: Harper, 1972.

Lavender, David S. *California: A Bicentennial History.* New York: Norton, 1976.

Loftis, Anne. *California— Where the Twain Did Meet.* New York: Macmillan, 1973.

Rolle, Andrew F. *California: A History,* 2nd ed. New York: Crowell, 1969.

Rolle, Andrew F., and Gaines, J. S. *The Golden State: A History of California,* 2nd ed. AHM, 1979.

Sanderlin, George W. *The Settlement of California.* New York: Coward, 1972.

Starr, Kevin. *California! A History.* Peregrine Smith, 1980.

Suggs, Robert C. *The Archaeology of San Francisco.* New York: Crowell, 1965.

Terrell, John U. *The Discovery of California.* New York: Harcourt, 1970.

Hawaii

Bianchi, Lois. *Hawaii in Pictures.* Sterling, 1979.

Carpenter, Allan. *Hawaii,* rev. ed. Chicago: Childrens Press, 1979.

Fradin, Dennis B. *Hawaii in Words and Pictures.* Chicago: Childrens Press, 1980.

Gray, Francine du P. *Hawaii: The Sugar-Coated Fortress.* New York: Random House, 1972.

Joesting, Edward. *Hawaii: An Uncommon History.* New York: Norton, 1972.

Kane, Robert S. *Hawaii, A to Z Guide.* Rand McNally, 1981.

Simpich, Frederick, Jr. *Anatomy of Hawaii.* New York: Coward-McCann, 1971.

Wallace, Robert. *Hawaii.* New York: Time Inc., 1973.

Photo Credits/Acknowledgments

Photos on pages 3 (top), 5, courtesy of California Secretary of State; pages 3 (bottom), 41-43, 45, 47-48, 53-59, courtesy of Hawaii Visitors Bureau (pages 42-43, Peter French, page 47, Dan R. Salden, pages 48, 57, Warren Bolster, page 54, Greg Vaughn, page 59, Anthony Anjo); pages 6-7, 16, courtesy of Los Angeles Convention & Visitors Bureau; page 9 courtesy of Sacramento Convention & Visitors Bureau; pages 11, 17, courtesy of James Blank; pages 12-14, 50-51, courtesy of New York Public Library; pages 15, 30, courtesy of Tournament of Roses; page 18 courtesy of San Francisco Convention & Visitors Bureau; pages 19-20, 27, courtesy California Office of Tourism; page 21 courtesy of Mann's Chinese Theatre; page 2, courtesy of the Queen Mary; page 23 courtesy of Winners' Circle Ranch; page 24 courtesy of Winchester Mystery House; pages 25, 31, courtesy of Santa Barbara Convention & Visitors Bureau; page 26 courtesy of Universal City Studios (Peter C. Borsari); page 27 courtesy of Marine World-Africa US; page 29 courtesy of Gilroy Garlic Festival (Bill Strange); page 32 courtesy of Old Globe Theatre; page 35 courtesy of Hearst San Simean (John Blades); page 36 courtesy US Department of Housing and Urban Development; page 38 courtesy of the New York Mets; page 61 courtesy of NASA.

Cover photograph courtesy of San Francisco Convention & Visitors Bureau.